PI

THE STO.

"My life is like a light flickering, no longer hiding in the dark," writes the poet Fiona. Hers is one of a chorus of remarkable voices in *The Story of My Heart.* With honesty and courage, these young writers tell of struggles with abuse, addiction, mental illness. And yet, the poems gathered here also speak of strength and resilience, a will to go on *"even when life crumbles like broken bottles."* The work of Pongo and programs like it is vital, a testament to the healing powers of poetry. The poet Sasha writes, *"The story of my heart is so high and shiny, only eagles hear it. Deep and velvety—moles wear it tunneling home."*

ELLEN BASS, MA, Poet, Editor, Author of Indigo; Co-author of The Courage to Heal: A Guide for Women Survivors of Sexual Abuse

"CSTC Staff and I are so grateful for Pongo and The Story of My Heart. Our youth writers are so earnestly eager to have a listening community with which to share their understandings, their pains, their stories and their own complex and splendid yearnings. The Pongo mentors have also helped train our team (recreation therapists, nurses, counselors, psychologists, and physicians) to incorporate Pongo's narrative methods into a breadth of healing strategies for our work with youth. What gifts these young writers and their poems are!"

MICHAEL (MICK) STORCK, M.D. Attending Psychiatrist at Child Study & Treatment Center (CSTC); Associate Professor, Department of Psychiatry and Behavioral Sciences, University of Washington School of Medicine

The Story of My Heart

OTHER BOOKS OF PONGO TEEN POETRY

The Story of My Heart

**PONGO POETRY FROM CHILD
STUDY AND TREATMENT CENTER**

FALL 2010-SPRING 2020

Founder:
Richard Gold

Project Leader:
Ann Teplick

Executive Director:
Barbara Green

Development Manager:
Nebeu Shimeles

Program Manager:
Shaun McMichael

Assistant Project Leaders:
Eli Hastings, Ashley Skartvedt, Emily Holt,
Corey Teasdell, Erin Carpenter

Poetry Mentors:
Rebecca Maison-Diop, Alex Leviton,
Heather Timken, Nadia Imafidon,
Stephanie McManus, Roxanne Hulton,
Samantha Krejcik, Spencer Whalstrom,
Jaspar Lepak, Melanie Noel, Natalie
Singer-Velusch, Sandra Scannell, Katelyn
Durst, Gem Schaudies, Jasleena Grewal,
Nathaniel Orwiler, Lisa Madelle Bottomley,
Urvasi Graham, Anni Armas Mahoney,
Brittany Dennison, Jean Lenihan

PONGO POETRY PROJECT
Seattle, WA, June 2021

PONGO
POETRY PROJECT

Published in June 2021, by

PONGO PUBLISHING, INC.
153 14th Ave, #5
Seattle, WA 98122
www.pongoteenwriting.org
programmanager@pongoteenwriting.org

Cover Art: "From Ashes" by CSTC YOUTH ARTIST, JANE
Book Design: DANIA ZAFAR
Editor: ANN TEPLICK
Consulting Editor: RICHARD GOLD
Managing Editor: SHAUN ANTHONY MCMICHAEL

Image Credits
Decorative bird © KrimKate/iStock.com
Heart watercolor © Kateryna Kovarzh/iStock.com

Printed and bound in the United States of America

Dedicated to all Pongo Poets

Thanks to the following grantors for their generous support of the Pongo Poetry Project and this publication:

4Culture; City Of Seattle, Office Of Arts & Culture; Fales Foundation Trust; Ibis Foundation Of Arizona; Onefamily Foundation; Virginia Mason Health System; Washington State Arts Commission; Win & Terry Van Pelt; Luke & Felicia Van Pelt; Dawson & Laura Van Pelt; Paul & Charlene Cox

CONTENTS

School Year 2017-2018

My Hummingbird Heart 39

School Year 2016-2017

Love Is as Tender as a Wounded Dove 53

School Year 2015-2016

Myself as a Flower 71

School Year 2014-2015

Because I Didn't Have that Comfort 93

PREFACE

ANN TEPLICK
Pongo Poetry Project Lead
Child Study Treatment Center (CSTC)
2005-Present

"My heart is boiling water./It used to be bullet-riddled./
It will now become the slow and steady beat of a marathon runner"
(54/55).

The Story of My Heart is the story of the hearts of young people that
illuminate courage, resilience, and hope. The hearts of youth whose
journeys are epic, as the result of profound developmental and social
challenges. It's the story of hearts that have been stressed by insecure
families, losses upon losses, substance abuse, and life on the streets.
Hearts that try to erase the ache of abandonment, self-harm, and
suicidal ideation. Hearts that know the trickiness of trust and love.
"To get to love, you have to go through a minefield" (41). Hearts
wounded by abuse. "You took my innocence.../...I cried for you to
stop/but you didn't listen" (15). Many of these hearts have struggled
to discover their beauty and self-worth, having been socialized in a
racially oppressive society. These are children and teens who long
for families and homes that are loving, safe, and secure.

The hearts in this collection hold gratitude for being acknowl-
edged and listened to. "When someone deeply listens to me,/the knot
in my abdomen begins to loosen" (23). They know the importance
of self-respect, as difficult as that may be to attain. They express

1

the words they need to hear to keep them above water. "You are perfect just the way you are" (44). These hearts guide us with their fearlessness, truth, and wisdom. Theirs are the words they need to share, and we need to hear.

Since 2000, the Pongo Poetry Project has facilitated poetry writing workshops for children and teens at Child Study & Treatment Center (CSTC), the only state-run psychiatric hospital for youth in Washington State. The youth in residence range in age from 6-17 and stay for an average of 8 months. They have been diagnosed with a variety of conditions including traumatic stress, developmental and learning disabilities, and autism. Though roughly 40% of the youth arrive at CSTC due to a court order, by the end of their stay, nearly all youth are voluntary residents.

It's an honor to be Pongo's Project Lead at CSTC. I work with Pongo mentors, who are adult volunteers trained in the Pongo methods. Some of the poems are written in free verse, dictated to a Pongo mentor to record. Others are inspired by well-chosen writing activities which allow for a variety of structures to fit the needs of all writers. We engage students in the writing, on campus, at Oak Grove School, a public elementary; and Firwood School, a public middle and high school. We also write in the three residential cottages: Orcas, Ketron, and Camano. Close collaboration with staff at each of these sites anchors our project.

Do Pongo writers continue to write following their discharge from CSTC? In 2012, interviews with 36 former CSTC-Pongo participants found that:

- 78% said that Pongo had made a difference in their lives.
- 83% said that they still write.
- 72% attributed their participation in Pongo as the reason why they were still writing.

The work is not easy due to the anguish and grief in many of the stories. Early on, it was not uncommon for me to cry in the car on my way home. Cry when I had long been home. Lie awake recounting words I had heard, as I asked myself how does one receive narratives that contain an abundance of pain, uncertainty, and bewilderment? How does one absorb the sights and sounds we witness? And why have the misfortunes of life fallen on these brilliant, exuberant, and thoughtful young people? This work has taught me to walk strong and decisive. To walk humble. To walk the walk of mindfulness where I practice being present, no matter how uncomfortable I am. And to listen with a depth I had never known. As well, I have learned to recognize my own vulnerabilities and not be ashamed.

At Pongo, we believe that those who live delicate, layered, and complicated lives, have important things to say, and that the world needs their stories. We believe these stories allow us to better understand one another and open our hearts. We believe self-expression through art helps us to make sense of ourselves and our worlds and that a poem is the perfect container to hold our emotions and feelings.

We are advocates for voices that far too often are overlooked. We share our love for poetry and the tools for writing a poem from the heart. These poems offer relief, satisfaction, pride, and a higher sense of purpose and self. We witness this when, after writing, young people's body posture straightens while hoods lift from their faces. After writing, youth make easier eye contact, and their smiles widen. We see this in their eagerness to share their poems, no matter how unsettling the theme.

The poet Rumi said, "The quieter you become, the more you are able to hear." At Pongo, we lean into waves of chaos that often involve deep-rooted trauma. We listen without judgment.

We applaud the courage of these poets to investigate and celebrate who they are, as they share what resides at the core of each of us—a desire to be loved and understood.

"My heart is so big, it needs a 5-story mansion" (118).

The 104 poems in this collection are organized in sections by the years they were written. The poets' names and some of the details in their poetry have been changed for confidentiality.

I would like to acknowledge the many people who have made Pongo's work possible at CSTC:

I begin at the beginning, with Richard Gold – Pongo's Founder, cherished friend, and guide. I am grateful to have been mentored by Richard these last twenty years. And to have learned, through his modelling, how to be human with kindness, generosity, integrity, and grace. He has called on me to put my best foot forward, no matter what, and especially when the terrain is rugged. I hold this through all aspects of my life.

I thank the CSTC "village" that makes our program a success: the Pongo mentors, past and present; the Recreation Therapy Team; the schools; the directors, supervisors, psychiatrists, and others who work with youth at the residential cottages; and CSTC's administration. These include Angel Beckford, Tony Bowie, Paul Bowyer, Dr. Lee Carlisle, Erin Carpenter, Dr. Fran Dewalt, Lauren Edwards, Dr. Michelle Giresi, Raewyn Heim, Cody Jones, Dr. Liz Jordan, Dr. Jon Kuniyoshi, Sarah Magdanz, Dr. Jack McClelland, Shaun McMichael, Dr. Jeremy Norris, Terri Parks, Anna Seiler, Dr. Michael Storck, Corey Teasdell, and Carolyn Watkins.

My warmest appreciation, as well, to our team of proofreaders: Alex Leviton, Nicole Pomeroy, Gemlene Schaudies, and Ashley Skartvedt.

If reading this collection inspires you to learn more about Pongo's 25-year-long story, we invite you to:
- Visit Pongo's website: https://www.pongoteenwriting.org
- Download free writing activities and submit poetry on our website.

- Learn about training and volunteer opportunities by emailing *programmanager@pongoteenwritring.org*
- Purchase a copy of Founder Richard Gold's book, *Writing with At-Risk Youth: The Pongo Teen Writing Method* (Rowman & Littlefield Education, 2014), a field guide to starting a poetry writing project.
- Donate by visiting our website or emailing *developmentmanager@pongoteenwriting.org*

Thank you!

The Most Real I Feel

FROM ASHES
Jane, age 17

Where Are the Stars?

Long car rides with stars filling our eyes
My heart full of childish dreams
No destination, just going to go
Queen, Journey, AC/DC & Backstreet Boys
playing loud
Loud like an infinite echo

Out of nowhere, almost like a crash
it came to a stop
The stars faded out of my eyes, and I realized
that your eyes
had always been empty

You made a promise and sealed it with *I love you*
What happened to that promise?
What happened to *I love you*?

The words rang in my ears as I closed my eyes
hoping this wasn't real
Tears flooded down my cheeks
until I cried every tear I had

Yelling, screaming, crying, pushing you away
as you sat there and stole from me
You took my innocence, my heart, my love
Everything I cared about seemed to be gone
as I cried for you to stop
You didn't listen

Numb from pain
Denial
How could this happen?
I realized it happened because I trusted you
when I got in the car
It was all my fault
In that car, you stole my innocence
and left me broken
hurt
and damaged
on the side of the road

What happened to the stars in my eyes?

What happened to my childish dreams?

Dedicated to anyone who's ever had the stars taken from their eyes

An Unwanted Friend

At first,
I was afraid to be with you.
I knew my family wouldn't like you.
I knew we had entirely different friends
and yet
I started hanging around your crowd
and that's when we became better friends.

With each time I hung out with you
we became closer and closer
and the more I felt
I needed to be with you.

All of my time and money
became focused on you,
I stole for you,
I lied for you,
I snuck around my family for you
and that's when I knew
I was addicted.

LAWRENCE, age 17

A Thanksgiving Carol

Back then I was a pretty messed-up kid
Back then I had anger problems
Back then I had temper tantrums
Back then I had to be restrained
Back then I was in special classes in normal schools
Back then I was abusive
Back then I punched glass
Back then I got sent to the hospital
Back then I moved
Back then I got sent to anger behavioral school
Back then I experienced loss

Now I am better
Now I hardly hit on purpose
Now I go to therapy that works
Now I am looking forward to the future

In the future I will write comedy
In the future I will get married
In the future I will have kids
In the future I will become a grandfather
In the future I will die happy

Dedicated to my mom, dad, and aunt

Tick, Tick, Tick

The clock's relentless mantra reminds me
that I don't have time
to consider the passing hours
that pile up on each other like slips of paper,
each delicately holding the name of a faded soul.

Who am I? Who was I? I stand
at the edge of a dock watching the still silhouette
of my past self, sinking into the abyss of human faults
and tears of lost lovers.

We can fill an ocean.

Tick, tick, tick. It burns through the surface of my ears.
It's practically shouting—*stop sitting there*
gawking at the never-ending spiral
of judgment and neglect
we call society!
Get up there and... Tick, tick, tick.
It won't finish. It's beckoning.
Just say something.

How much time have I wasted? I stand
glued to the floor
as if roots were sprouting from my feet,
interlocking with the soil.
I wish I could feel the embrace that's around me.
But for now, all I can feel, all I can hear is
tick, tick, tick.

Emotional Rollercoaster

I'm discharging soon.
It's very, very scary.

I was on the streets before I came here
getting sexually assaulted
and beaten
and I'm not used to going to a new placement
because I was with this great foster parent
until she chose not to be my foster mom
and this felt like a sad situation
that I could never get over.

I'm going to a group home.
It's very, very scary,
because I'm meeting new people,
and who knows if they're good or bad.

Changes can be hard.

Changes can also be painful.

I've been through a lot
that's made me realize
that I don't want to become like my mom—
a drug addict, going to parties all the time
getting high, sexually assaulted,
and beaten.
I also don't want to become like my dad—
joining gangs
and beating and sexually assaulting people.

I want to make my own good life out of it
and help people.
I want to make a challenge for myself
by fighting for other people.

I would like the people at the new group home
to know something about me—
that I've been through a lot
and I don't want the same thing to happen again.

Dedicated to my foster mom

When Someone Really Listens to Me[1]

They understand that I need to talk,
and I feel gratitude.
I feel like I'm flying through a blue, sunny sky,
letting the clouds of past hate leave my soul,
feeling all the rude remarks melt away
like ice cream on a hot summer day,
welcoming waves of love and support
into my life,
like an ocean of happiness crashing
onto a land of war and anger,
bringing peace for the moment being.

When someone really listens to me,
I feel a connection
that makes me feel safe and seen,
even if life is hard.
Things are going to be okay.

---

1 After "When Someone Deeply Listens to You" by John Fox

When someone really listens to me,
they hear my words, not clouded or distorted.
They will see the forgiveness I desire.
When someone really listens to me,
I feel warm and welcomed
and that I'm exactly where I am supposed to be.

When someone really listens to me,
it's the most real I feel.
I feel wanted and loved and worthy.

When someone really listens to me,
the knot in my abdomen begins to loosen
like a pile of tangled yarn.
It wraps in a ball
ordered, light,
quiet,
and ready.

On Tanner's YouTube Channel

I don't have a YouTube Channel
but if I did, I would wear
the craziest ties ever.
I can't wear ties here,
but at home, that's how I express myself.

Sometimes they express how I feel.
Sometimes they're just there to be funny.
Yet they're always different
than everyone else's.

I got ties with cats—
some are tubby, some are not.
Some are lying, some are sleeping
while some are prowling the night's sky.
The times I wear my cat ties
are when I'm feeling mischievous or sly.

I've got ties with dots and ties with stripes.
Some colors match, and some colors don't.

I've got dino nugget ties—
those obviously are worn when I'm hungry.
I've got taco ties, hot dog ties, burger ties too.
Avocado ties are by far my favorite!

On my YouTube Channel, these ties
would not just express myself
but they would also express
what fun stuff we're doing that day.

If I wore sports ties,
that day I would show off
how terrible I am at basketball.

If I wore ties with books, I would show
how little I know about famous authors.
If I wore ties with beakers and vials
I could show everyone that I'm alright at science.
The one tie I would love to wear the most
would be my math tie
yet I feel I'd get the least amount
of views on those episodes.

In the end though,
I don't feel it matters
what people think about me
or my ties.
I wear my ties
not for what other people think I should feel
but for what I want to feel.

Keep Fighting for What's Right for You

I am full of dangerous and loyal—
full of proud and compassionate.
I am shy and understanding.
I try to be strong and helpful,
caring and loving
but I always end up on the ground.

I try to help and be kind to people
but all they do is beat me
and leave scars on my face,
leaving me to bleed to death.
I try with all my might to defend myself
but all they do is criticize and mock me.

Sometimes I reflect myself in the mirror
and see "unwanted person."

I just don't understand the world.

I try to forget about the past
but I always grudge on, never letting it go
until I feel like getting revenge on them.

But then I realize
that I am strong and caring.
It's not easy
but at least I can still try.
Sometimes I feel like the whole world is on me—
that it gets heavier and heavier
until I cannot walk anymore.

But somebody told me once
keep fighting the good fight
and never give up.

My Motivation

My motivation
is watching the cars on the highway,
imagining that one day,
I'll be in one of them, on the way home.

We're going to be planting an apple tree,
hoping that when I come home, it will bloom.
It represents a new springing of life.
It will be like starting a new life at home,
instead of at a treatment center.

I feel excited for a new welcoming
to the place that I always remember
and the things that mean the most to me
like my pets and family.
The feeling is like a new wave overturning the old.
Like we're moving on in a new life.

I want to be able to overturn the old
and express the feelings inside.
Instead of being a dead seed in the ground,
I want to be springing forward
and rising up like a giant oak tree in the sky.

Once I'm home, I definitely want
to give my dog the biggest belly rub ever.
I want to be able to feel peace on the couch,
cuddling with my cat,
and being wrapped in my mom's arms.
I want to walk on the side of the lake with my dad
and watch the waves slowly rise
as the winds come through.

I want to feel welcomed in the community around me,
to walk through nature, to feel the winds again
and see the camp that means so much to me.
Most of all, I want to be with my family—
the one that hopes and cares most for me.
My excitement is for these two months
to be able to pass over,
and rise up like a new wave and ride home.

Dedicated to my family and to camp

The Power of Family

The power of family
is the way they hug you,
wrap you in their arms
and whisper, *It's gonna be okay.*

The power of family is
the way they're there
when no one else is
through the hardest of times,
the worst of times,
all the times.

The power of family
is when you have an emotion
no one else seems to have
that seems to carry over
to the family members
that are right around you.

The power of family
can defeat an opponent
easily, without a struggle.

The power of family
is the strongest power
ever invented.

I Promise, I'm Sorry

Even when life crumbles
like broken bottles under my feet
When it shatters like undone dreams
Even when my throat is filled
with the screams I hide under my smile
When my throat is filled with the words
I've held in for a while
Even as my lungs reach for a break
as I'm running this ongoing chase
Even when my heart breaks under the things
I've seen and heard
Even when my hands ball into a fist
hurting everyone around me
pushing through the past that binds me
even so, I will hold you, life

I will push on
Not for myself
but for those who need not see me fail
I will hold you, life
as if you were the last thing
anchoring me to shore
and I will say I'm sorry
I promise to try again

---

2   After "The Thing Is" by Ellen Bass

We Dream for the World

GIRL
Valencia, age 12

I Am the Girl with the Problems

I am the girl who has a heart condition.
I am the girl who will probably scream
at the top of her lungs.
I am the girl with the syndrome.
I am the girl that everyone hates.
I am the girl who people think does not care.
But under all these issues
that people are gunning me for,
know that I care more than people think.
I long to have friends.
I want people to know
that my disabilities
are a part of me
but aren't me.

Why?

Why were you never there?
Why did you leave me?
Why won't you tell me where you were?

Where were you?
Where did you go?
Where did you leave me?

How long did you leave me?
How could you leave me?
How come you weren't there?

Who did you leave me with?
Who was there for me?
Who wasn't there for me?

When did you leave?
When did you go?
When will you be back?

What did you do?
What were you thinking?
What did I do?

Why?

Running

When I was really little, I ran away
from people trying to tackle me in football
I was afraid of my mom
At the time, I ran under my bed
I dreamt about outer space

When I got a little older, I ran away
from people trying to tag me in tag
At the time, I ran toward my older brother
When I ran, I hoped for safety
and I got it

Today when I run, I run away
from people on drugs and alcohol
More than anything, I wish
I could run away from my mom
Today when I run, I run toward
the football field or basketball hoop
More than anything,
I wish I could run back home

Sometimes I Feel Like...

Sometimes I feel like
a paperclip
stuck with nothing to do

Sometimes I feel like
a fish in a fishbowl
circling with nowhere to go

Sometimes I feel like
a little kid trapped in a basement
by my neighbor

Sometimes I feel like
this story is coming to an end

Helping Heart

I made a speech in my room once
about people who are suicidal.

First,
why would you do that?
Do you think everybody else would be happy?
Do you have loved ones that care?
If you don't, then what's the point
of listening to this?
Everybody has loved ones in their life.
Even if you think they don't care.
They are somewhere out there in the world.
Maybe hiding in the shadows away from you.
Somewhere in their heart, they may love you.

Second,
you may be depressed
because you've been bullied or abused.
Everybody has a reason for those things
but sometimes their reasons
aren't good enough for you.

Everybody has someone
but sometimes that someone can't be trusted.
It's kind of like being in a pool,
putting water through your hands
but it doesn't stay.
If this has ever happened to you
maybe you could get some help
because everybody needs help sometimes.

Getting help feels like a sunny day,
breaking through you even though it is fall.
Even though
you think there is a greener side to the grass,
it's just not true.
Everybody is on the green side,
even though they might not realize it.

Dedicated to people who feel like this is true

Don't Do Drugs

Why? Because they are bad for you. For example, cigarettes and heroin. Heroin gives you blood diseases because of needles. Cigarettes put tar in your lungs and give you cancer.

I know this because my mom does a lot of this. She has used heroin, cigarettes, crack, Molly, marijuana, and meth. Those things got her in a lot of trouble. She got involved with the police and has been in and out of jail since I was 4. She started when she was 12. And because of all the stuff she does, she's influenced me to use the stuff she did. I used marijuana, but I quit. Then my sister put me in CSTC, and that's helped a lot 'cause I tried to stab a cop while I was on drugs. I hope the cop sees this poem. I'm sorry.

When you are picking drugs, you are picking drugs over your family. You never know, you could die. You're practically killing yourself, so quit. Make good choices.

Sincerely,
Travis

Getting Through the Minefield of Love

To get to love, you have to go through a minefield
The ground is red from people who tried to get through
but failed
The sky is gray because of the mines going off
Blue is tears on a person's face
because they may never get through alive
Black is determination to get through and not give up
Green is you getting through the field
Yellow is happiness that you got through alive
Orange is you and your love at a sunset
Pink is you with your family
Purple is you losing everything
and having to start all over
Tan is you thinking you could never do it again

Dedicated to my family

My Dream for the World

I dream of a world
where each individual perspective is respected.
Where there are no gunshots fired.
Where there are no haters.
Where there are no bullies.
I dream of a world where there is no fighting,
and no people being so mean
to other kids that they commit suicide.
I dream there are no drug overdoses
and no sexist or fascist jokes.
I also don't want Black people being treated badly
because of their skin color.
I dream of a world
where there are more animal welfare groups.
Where everyone gets along.
Where I get to meet all the rappers!
Where I get all the Jordans in the world.
(There is Jordan cologne!)
I dream of a world where
we can all be more comfortable
and enjoy learning from one another.

Life at Home

I'm from a place where lies will spill
I'm from a place where my family tries their best
When I'm upset, they'll pray for me
I'm from the pink scars that cover my body
I'm from the slimy kisses that my two dogs give me
I'm from the ragged clothes I skateboard in
I'm from a place where I have fun hanging out
with my family and making jokes
I'm from a home where tears are spilled
I'm from the boat that me and my dad fish in
for salmon and rainbow trout
I'm from the warm, cozy hugs
that my mom gives me when I'm upset
I'm from the hospital I got sent to
so my mom and dad could help me
I'm from the tasty, spicy chicken
that my sister makes me
I'm from the new video games I played
that my smart sister showed me
I'm from the Christian music that helps me calm down
I'm from the family I love

Dedicated to my family

These Are the Words I Need to Hear

I love you
Be yourself
I want you to be happy
Meow
Purr
You are so handsome
You are the greatest
I hope you stay the same
You have a good heart
You are perfect just the way you are

Dedicated to my mom and dad

My Hummingbird Heart

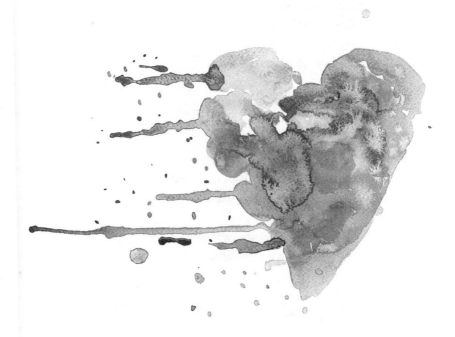

What I Feel Inside

I want you to see how you can hurt me.
I want you to know what it's like
when a person is honest.
I want you to know how I feel
when you break my trust—
like getting stabbed in the heart.

I want you to understand my pain
when I get bullied.

I want you to know how I express myself.
My words are like the animals in the ocean—
bottlenose dolphins and killer whales.

I want you to know what I am capable of.
My strength is like oxygen from the trees.

I want you to know my heart.
My love is like parents to a child.

Dedicated to my family

Love is Fake

I have too much experience
with love not going well.

My mom loved heroin
more than she loved me
or anyone else.

My sister's boyfriend wanted sex
more than consent
or caring about the fact that I was 6.

My adopted father didn't care
enough to stop drinking, even though
it was leaving me with bruises.

My adopted parents care
more about their son being perfect
than seeing that he's not okay.

So, this is why
I have no faith in love.

Pain in the Darkness

I am painting my self-portrait.
For this work, I have chosen
red for my rage,
black for my darkness,
and green for my disgust.
The background of my self-portrait will have fire
because my life has been full of pain.

In my self-portrait, I will be holding a knife,
because the sharp pain
is the most important thing in my life.
In my self-portrait, my eyes
will look like snake eyes.

I would like to give my self-portrait to myself
because I appreciate the way I am.

Dedicated to Mom

Violence in the Sense

Violence. Smells like gasoline—
a lawnmower that just blew up.
It smells like the brussels sprouts in the oven
burning to ash.
It smells like clothing covered in mildew.

Violence. Tastes like Sour Patch Kids mixed
with tequila and dog urine.
Tastes like hot sauce mixed with coal.
Like horse hooves mixed with rotten creamed corn
and moldy horseradish.

Violence. Sounds like screams coming from a child
trying to get help for his mother who's getting beaten.
Sounds like cries for help from a dog
getting attacked by a coyote.

Violence. Feels like razorblades
slicing across my calves.
Feels like getting tetanus from a rusty knife.
Feels like a cut that's gotten infected
and getting gangrene.

Dedicated to my mom and sister

If My Fist Could Speak

If my fist could speak,
it would tell you that I've hurt people.

If my fist could speak, it would recall the looks
on people's faces before I hit them—scared
like someone holding your mom at gunpoint.

If my eyes could speak, they would tell you
about the deep pain I've caused,
which feels like a disappointment.

If my pounding heart could speak, it would say
I'm aching from top to bottom,
wishing I could take it all back.

If my hair could speak, it would explain
I'm hiding behind it
because I'm hiding as much as I can.

If my ears could speak,
they would share all the screams
that I've heard and all the *please, don't.*
It's sad.
Like losing someone
and they're never coming back.

If my body could speak, it would tell you about how
I don't look like much is going on, on the outside
but on the inside,
there's a lot going on.

If my brain could deal with everything,
it would want to ask why I do it
and why I can't stop.

Blessings

This is for the person who never smiles
    It's easy to be unhappy
    It's easy to be happy
    But it's hard to put a true, natural smile on your face
This is for the old man drawing a sidewalk picture
    of a gardenia, with red chalk
For the mom who lost her kids because of drugs
    and getting hit. She needed to hear *I love you*
    just to know she exists
    I felt bad when I left. It made me want to cry
    Even drove me to the point of suicide
This is for the square pegs in round holes
    For children catching baby frogs
    and putting them in their pencil cases before school
This is for the wide-eyed child, whose biggest life choice
    is pizza or nuggets
For the mom who works tirelessly, daily
    to give her child the world
For the dad who may or may not be around
For the future
This is for the girl who is afraid
    to get out of bed every morning
    and may lie lifeless for hours at a time
    Pray tomorrow greets her like a soft fleece blanket
    in a reading nook

This Is for the Girls Like Me

This is for the girls who think they're ugly. This is for the girls who think they're fat. This is for the girls who have had abusive parents. This is for the girls who feel drugs and alcohol are the only way out. This is for the girls who have been taken advantage of, raped, and hurt. This is for the girls who struggle with depression and low self-esteem. This is for the girls like me. This is for the girls who have a hard time believing they're worth a simple dime and put in time. This is for the girls who have lost something.

My Heart

My heart is beautiful and alive and ready to move on.
It used to be hurt and broken all the way through.
It will become like NYC
where everybody wants to live.
My heart is strong because I put it down a lot.
I am getting better.

My heart knows who I am on the inside and out.
It feels like I'm worth it.
My heart used to be like a poor, abused little animal
with no one to look after it.
My heart is boiling water.
It used to be bullet-riddled.
It will become the slow and steady beat
of a marathon runner.
It is strong, like a lotus.

My heart knows the resiliency of hummingbirds.
It feels there are second chances.
It will become strong and whole and do whatever it takes
to get to the other side of the hole in the road.
My heart is the sun at 5:30 in the evening,
still present and warm, streaming colors across the sky,
but exhausted from labor.

My heart used to be a walnut, incredibly tough—
almost impossible to open, but once cracked,
a complete mess inside.
My heart will become a djembe—beating strong
and pulsating through everyone who is around.

My heart is optimistic—always half full.
It used to be easily influenced.
It will become older but wiser.

My heart is beautiful.
My heart knows I've done wrong,
but it also knows I can fix things
and go on with my life
and make sure it is a good one.

When I Grow Up, I'll Be a Hero

I can't wait to be an adult.
I'm going to be like my heroes—like MLK.
I'm going to do peaceful protests, make speeches
and visit places in hard times.

I'll write letters to the president,
win the Nobel Peace prize,
and if I get to, I'll thank my grandma, my teacher
and of course, Pongo.

If I had to die for a good cause,
it would be to stop trafficking.
Maybe people would stop being sexists
and homophobic
and trafficking and assaulting women,
because it is wrong.

When I watch the news and hear about people protesting
trafficking and school shootings,
that makes me want to help.

I want to yell, *I hate violence.*
I wish there was world peace
but that won't happen.

I cry when people and friends get hurt or killed
like when my best friend's dad got shot
when someone wanted his money for drugs.

I will fight for peace
but not with violence—
I will fight peacefully.

Dedicated to my grandmas

Reasons to Love Me

I may not be perfect,
but I can help endangered cheetahs!
I always wish for the peace
Martin Luther King Jr. gave the world.
I do my best to understand injustice:
people on the streets don't need to be beat up every day.
I have unusual ideas like creating my dream house
to be big and cozy, so I feel safe.
I want the people around me to feel justice,
harmony, and peace.

I hold onto some things forever,
like my mom's wedding ring
from when her last husband died in a car accident.
I keep it with Grandpa's ashes,
Snickerdoodle's cat toys
and Mom's lucky rock.

If I were an animal, I'd be a cheetah and run
into sunsets and beaches.
I have a secret talent. I can do gymnastics
and put my feet behind my head.
I am special.

Dedicated to my family and the editor

Love Is as Tender as a Wounded Dove

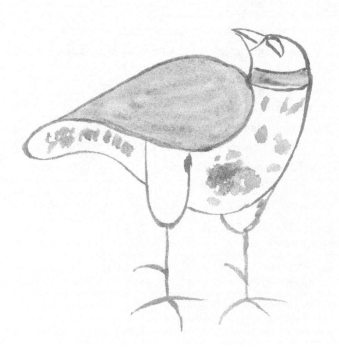

Questions for My Dad

Why weren't you there for me?
When are you going to come back?
Where are you? Who are you?
Do I want to try to get to know you if you come back?
Do I know you?
Are you dead? Are you alive?
Why don't you come back to our family?
Why don't you get to know your own son and daughter?

I run from home.
I run away to go do drugs.
Why do I like this feeling?
Why do I have this sense that I hate it?
Why do I hurt those around me,
those who are closest to me?
The father figures that I do have...
They are there for me.
They care about me.
They love me.
If you are my dad,
why don't you care about me, love me?

Erase

I wish I could erase my past, most or all
Make it seem foggy
like how you erase something on paper
until the pink stuff comes off in little snakes
but no matter how hard you try
you will always have some of the words

I wish I could erase how I treat people
Maybe how I teach or learn
I wish I could erase the scars
on my stomach and wish I could erase
what I say to people, 'cause honestly
I treat people like crap

I wish I could erase my friend dying
on my birthday

I wish I could erase my mom
not being there for me

I wish I wouldn't have to wish
to erase

Dear Mom

Listen to my story—

You should know that if you're struggling,
you are not alone.
There are others out there struggling
with similar situations or the same problems as you.
And when I say problems, I don't mean it in a mean way—
I mean it in a true, welcoming-in-your-treatment way.

Listen to my story—

The days were long and cold—
long like a bridge, cold like a winter breeze.
I heard the pills in the background, in my mother's room
shaking like a baby's rattle.
I saw her coming in and out of the house
with different people. And then they would leave.
And then one day, she left too.
I kept waiting by the doors, waiting.
I wish she would have listened to my story.

Listen to my story—

Now I come home from school.
I go into the bathroom and hide.
I feel like the world is ganging up on me.
I feel like cement walls are pressing me together
and pulling me apart.
I am hiding from the people who are angry at me.
I am hiding from my anxiety and depression.
My mom and dad and sister aren't here—I am alone.
I can tell my days are getting worse.

Listen to my story.

Dedicated to my loving sister

Can You Hear Me Yet?

I have two names
I don't like one
I'm judged, even hated
and all I did was be myself
No drugs—nothing like that
so I don't understand why it's so hard

I'm the youngest of nine siblings
My parents are my life
My friends, my future
My dogs, my best friend's baby girl
All loved dearly

I just met my mom this year
I was told my family all died
But there my mom was, waiting for me
on the porch at my aunt's house

What would I have done if I never met her?
I've been told so many lies about my family
The truth is
they're awesome

My parents had terrible lives
and they don't want me to end up the same

Too late for any of that

We aren't born knowing things
We are taught things
We see ourselves the way we want to see ourselves
I don't see myself the way I am

Where I'm From

Where I'm from, we don't got an easy life,
but it's our life.
Where I'm from, you learn how to break out
of handcuffs when you're 13.

Where I'm from, books are the only escape.
If you're lucky, you won't get caught reading.
Where I'm from, family may be the last thing you ever got.

Where I'm from, if you're 16 and never been arrested
you're gonna get turned out.

Where I'm from, friends feel like paradise.

Where I'm from, the front door stays open during the summer.
In the winter, the door's still open, but the fire's going.
Where I'm from, my mom says leaving the door open
means you're not all bad.

Where I'm from, the adults try not to drink,
saying life is perfect
and they don't want to ruin it.

Where I'm from, there ain't no Starbucks.
Where I'm from, life's okay.
Where I'm from, we play peek-a-boo with our nephews.
Where I'm from, you learn character at a young age.

Where I'm from, it may seem
like we're all bad on the outside.
On the inside,
we're just like everybody else.

Dedicated to my home

Running From Me

When I was really little, I ran from my mom's yelling
and her boyfriends' fists.
I was afraid of the violence,
the bruises, and the broken dreams.
At that time, I ran toward locked doors and smiling faces.
I dreamed about a new life, a new me.

When I got a little older, I ran from my mom's sickness
and her husband's fists.
When I ran, I expected that I'd get hurt if I stayed.
At the time, I ran toward my siblings
and their crying faces.
When I ran, I hoped for a different life and a different me.

Today when I run, I run away from my own head—
my flashbacks. More than anything
I wish I could run from my family and abuse.
Today, when I run, I run toward my medications
and my bed. More than anything
I wish I could run
to a different life,
a better life.

FIONA, age 17

Finding Light

My life is like a light flickering.
A bright lightbulb—angel white—
that's dying, but it's trying.
Bruises from being abused
and weakness from not eating
don't define me,
but they may drag me down.
Many of my demons grab hold of me
trying to show me the place where I belong.
Some days, I break free
like a rabbit breaking free from a trap,
trying to live another day,
with lots of laughing, adventuring,
finding the missing pieces
that are a part of me.
My life is like a light flickering,
no longer hiding in the dark,
but finding the light that will stay
for the rest of my life.

Dedicated to those who struggle finding light to go on everyday

My Heart

My heart is like a pineapple, sweet on the inside,
with tough skin and wild energy bursting from the top.
My heart is like a pool of water in the height of summer
that everyone wants to jump into.
It's like a fragile vase sitting at the edge
of an unstable bookcase.
It's like a forgotten well overgrown with moss,
a series of checks and balances, careful rules
put in place. A topography of buttes and prairies,
roughened and smoothed by forces outside
of man's reach.

My heart is like a glass bottle that will shatter
if you're not careful with it. It absorbs its environment.
If it is surrounded by ice, it shatters,
but when all is right,
it can be molded into something beautiful.
My heart is like heather blooming each fall.
It's a red heart. Black and blue. A rodeo bull.

I wish my heart could transform into an eagle, soaring free
I wish my heart was like the antlers of an elk—
firm, strong, capable, covered with soft fur.
I wish my heart was like a summer day—
calm, slow, fresh. A day when nothing can go wrong—
all of your problems a million miles away
and all is right.
I wish my heart was not so dark.
I wish my heart was warm.
I wish my heart was love.

I wish my heart was a closed book,
left for a forgotten self, coated in dust.
I wish it was like a resilient flower bulb
that is safe underground through the cold winter,
then sprouts and grows
into a beautiful, strong flower each spring.
I wish my heart was like a vault locked away
in an ice cave in Antarctica.
I wish it was like a giant ear that could listen
to people who disagree without getting angry.
I wish it was an open door that was always laughing.
A bird that could fly wherever it wanted, without
asking for permission.

To Chris/ From your Nephew, Marcus

I know you're a little vulnerable
because you lost a loved one.
May your heart become its own medicine,
so you could love another.
And just know, it's okay to cry.
May your heart become a whole heart
and not one that's broken.
May your heart become a sun aglow
so that it may brighten your day.
May your heart become an ocean wave,
so that you may forget all your troubles
and be like a surfer.
May your heart become a bowl
of chocolate ice-cream,
so that you're not so vulnerable
but full of joy.

Dedicated to my uncle

My Blessings

May the sun
shine on my brightness.

May the moonlight
guide me through my worries.

May my tarantula
not bite me when I feed him.

May the Pacific Ocean
splash my life with happiness.

May the grass
tickle my toes when I run through my garden.

May the polar bear's warm, fuzzy fur
keep me as warm as the Arctic sun at night.

May my new yellow Lab
snuggle with me when I sleep.

May the geese
fly freely so that I can smile.

Love

Love is tender as a wounded dove.
Love is something you can't hide.
Love is something special in life.

Love is not a word you just throw around.
It means more than that.

Love is a condition of care: unconditional.
Loving someone means you have to be there for them
when they need you most.

I've been there in that way.

Loving someone has to be for the right reasons.
You can't love someone for what they have
or what they look like.

You have to love someone for what they've been through
and what they've overcome.
For how they were the first day you met them.

The first day you meet someone is a moment
you never forget. You will remember it
for the rest of your life, that first impression.

Love feels like my heart is wrapped up
in a pink cashmere sweater.

Love is a thing that can be tattered
and shattered
but if it's real, not broken,
like a cracked window.

Love is me telling the world,
I have overcome my fears.

Blessed Into the World

Everyone has a blessing.
You may not feel it.
You may not think you have one,
but everyone has a blessing
being in the world.
The world is blessed to have you.
You may not feel it,
because you may be going through hard times,
like having your brother and sisters taken
away from family and put into foster homes,
or parents going through hard times, using drugs.
You may be going through hard times
but it's a blessing,
because you get to experience
things that other people may not.
Everyone's story is different,
and everyone has a story to tell.

Dedicated to the CSTC book of poems

Myself as a Flower

THE HEART OF LIFE
Valencia, age 12

My Pain

My pain is bigger than the sun but deep blue.
My pain is so heavy, it has broken my mind.
My pain is so deep, it's deeper than
       the most hidden part of the ocean.
My pain is so sharp it would cut the thickest skin.
My pain is so intense, it's like fire—
       burning through gasoline under my skin.
My pain is so out of control,
it's like a starving panther, pacing in too small a cage.
My pain is so overwhelming, it's a nuclear explosion.
My pain is familiar like a close friend.
My pain is always with me, closer than my skin.

My pain is so hard to describe.

I don't think anyone is listening.

When you read this poem, will you hear me?

Falling

I'm so stressed out.
My legs are tapping.
I am too warm.
My arms are weak.
My brain is thinking:

Going down:
    I don't know—
Plummeting:
    I don't know—
I need to stop:
    I don't know—

I need to cut.
I need to cut the stress.
When I cut, I'm relieved.
My legs shake less.
My temperature goes to normal.
My arms hurt
    (but that's where I cut)
My brain is slower.

Hitting bottom,
I feel better.

Love

Tired, sad, hungry, depressed, fucked
Screwed. Empty
This is how I've been feeling lately
Life just ain't going the way I want it to

Her
Every day someone mentions her
Exactly who I want to forget
but I can't forget her

Love
When you're in it, you don't want to go to sleep
because you want to be with her
When you're out of it, you don't want to go to sleep
because you'll dream of her
Also, I had my wisdom tooth pulled
Pressure. Pain that leads to everywhere and sinks in
But love is so much worse
It leads to scars, broken bones, reckless behaviors
Puts you in a facility
Shitty, nice, more shitty, depressed
I want a taco, a burrito, a grill, and a truck
I want to get in my truck and go

Dedicated to her

To Live Life for the Moment[3]

To love life, even when it crumbles
like crackers and shattering glass.
Even when your throat screams for help.
Even when your lungs gasp for the energy
to tell someone else they are right.

To love life, even when your hands ball into fists
and you're so angry you punch a wall.
Even when anger is inside your head
like a ball of fire
and your heart is pounding so hard
like you got shot
in the heart
with a bullet.

To love life, even when your heart cries
for someone you care about.

Dedicated to my aunt

---

3   After "The Thing Is" by Ellen Bass

Bravery

My bravery gets me in trouble.
I get in fights protecting the people I care about
and they blame themselves for the fights
which makes me feel like I'm in the deep ocean.
I'm drowning.

My bravery gets me the affection of others.
People think that they can trust me—
trust that I have their back.
If my bravery could speak, it would say calm down
because you'll get arrested over it
and ruin relationships and make your life harder.

My bravery is as black as a chalkboard.
My bravery sounds like a snap of something inside me
because something is breaking,
giving me the strength to speak.
My bravery is always hiding behind my emotions
and when the emotions move,
it moves with them.

Anxiety

Anxiety feels like something tight,
like a blanket wrapped around you
or being in an MRI machine.

Anxiety tastes like an earthworm-flavored jellybean.

Anxiety sounds like a powerful waterfall
taking over your mind.

Anxiety looks like an abstract piece of art
that's mushed together with a bunch of mixed colors.

Anxiety smells like opening a bag of Takis—
those spicy, rolled tortilla chips.
It plugs your nose,
so it's hard to breathe.

That is anxiety.

Dedicated to everyone with anxiety

Cries

I know this guy
who knew everything about me
He knew what I hated
and what I liked
He tried to keep me away
from everything happy
Tried to bring me closer
to sadness and anger

I tried to kill him with friendships
but he yelled at them and told them
to go away or else

He would never threaten them though
He would threaten me instead
bringing me to my knees
while I asked him to stop
not knowing that the only person
who could stop him was me

The weird thing about him is
he loved others so much
The person he hated
was just me

I haven't seen him in a while
but sometimes he still comes
Making me bruised
Making me ache

Sometimes I still can't ask him
to leave me alone

This man was my depression

Dedicated to Mom and Dad, all parents, and my old self

A Math Poem

Life is not an absolute value.
Not everything is positive.
Absolute value is something's distance
on the number line from zero.
Distance is always positive,
so taking the absolute value
will always result in a positive quantity.

We had been doing absolute value in Math.
I'm very advanced,
but I still have to participate in class.

It came back to me during Poetry.
Feelings are the graph of a long polynomial.
They go up and down and vary a lot.
I don't have to manage my feelings when they're happy.
When they're down,
I have to manage them.

When you dip below the X-axis
on the downside of emotions—
sad, fearful, the chemical adrenaline—
you can make yourself feel better
by eating an apple
or a pecan.
They're spicy, as in filled with spices,
that bring out a strong aroma.
Pecan is my favorite.
It's got a bit of crunch—
super sweet and rich.
It's just fantastic.
I love the food pie
and the math one
but as a symbol, I prefer tau.[4]

_____

4   19th letter of the Greek alphabet, having the value of 300

What If

What if there was no anger?
If there was no anger, people would be safer.
People wouldn't hurt others or themselves.
People wouldn't put down others, making them hurt.
People wouldn't attack others, putting themselves in jail.

What if there was no sadness?
If there was no sadness, people would speak their minds.
They would tell people what's wrong.
People would keep themselves safe and care.
If there wasn't sadness, people wouldn't put themselves down
by calling themselves ugly or fat.

What if there was no joy?
If there was no joy, then anger and sadness would rule.
People would think there was nothing to lose.
They would hurt people and themselves.
There would be no good memories, only bad ones.
There would be no laughing with friends
or talking with family.
There would only be crying and fighting.

I want there to be joy.

This is Who I Am

I am an owl, fluid, a candle flame,
the face you have to face, mirrored in your stare,
the enemy of your essence, ripping it to shreds.
I am complicated. I am a steel ball bouncing
between bells and flippers. I am a river otter.

I will grow to be happy by the bank of a river,
elastic, like a wildfire, the person no one expected.
A grapevine, a mountain with moss on my north side,
a sunflower in a field in Tuscany.

I believe that we are born in magic, to tell stories.
That my light and my path
will make a way for others.
That one day, everything falls apart.
That life is a beautiful storm,
that we need more humor in the world.
I believe in putting roots
deep into the earth's core.

E.D.

Fifteen minutes is not enough time
to tell them why I didn't eat today.
When I first got this eating disorder,
I felt like I was no longer alone—
like it was there holding my hand,
like I could finally get through life
because I wasn't alone.

Everyone tells me
I'm too fat to have an eating disorder.
One doctor even told me
he didn't care if I didn't eat,
because honestly,
I could use to lose a few pounds.

But they don't know what's going on in my head.
It's like World War III in there.
A team of demons, like shadows of football players,
are my enemies who tell me not to eat,
to throw up when I eat,
to throw up to the point that I pass out.

There are people on my side too.
They say they're here with me
and that I can do it
and that I won't have to do it alone.

But I often feel that my team will leave me
to fend for myself.
Like my mom did, who was doing drugs.
Like my sister did, who was doing drugs.

I was left by myself to cook.
I had to get myself out of bed for school.
I was 6.

Some days there is hope,
like there's light at the end of the tunnel.
Some days there is failure,
like I am left in a dark hole
and climb out of it.

But I wish there was more than just fifteen minutes
to tell people about it.

Dedicated to all people that struggle with E.D.

On Forgiveness

Forgiveness. It's hard to do,
because you have to start with yourself.
You have to think about all the times
you have failed somebody,
broken trust,
or missed an opportunity
that you should have seized.

Once you consider yourself,
then you think about those who have treated you badly,
who have hurt you, not appreciated you, not listened,
jumped to conclusions, cheated you, assumed.

Forgiveness is on the other side of a mountain.
The mountain is built of anger,
resentment and sadness.
Some people scale it easily. I'll take my time.

Forgive, but don't forget.
If you forget, you will be trampled.
Forgive to be free, from guilt, from grudges.
Forgive, to let in—not to curl up like an oak leaf.

To hear with new ears, perhaps a new heart.
Not to have those *remember when* thoughts wash up.
To make moments with, and not hide away.
To laugh and whisper to your brother an inside joke.
Maybe something from growing up—
like the dog named Wolf
or the old green chicken coup with the toilet in it.

Your brother's girl says she hasn't seen him laugh
or unwind like this in a while.
Perhaps his childish side got lost in salutes and uniforms.
And me—my childish side is out there
with the winter wind, waiting to be caught and taken.

Marathon of Seasons

I am running a 180-day marathon[5]
Getting better
Learning, growing
It's exhausting because
this is my second 180-day marathon

I feel angry and impatient having to run
I see thousands of people
who have come into my life
cheering me on
But when I'm down in the dumps
I see nobody
I'm barely dragging on the ground
It's pouring down rain
Cold and blistering
I can barely see the finish line

I can imagine what the finish line will be like
Somebody catching me, running out to me
Picking me up
Carrying me there
I am imagining happiness
A feeling of accomplishment rushing over me

---

5   In Washington State, 180 days is the length of a court-ordered treatment assignment for someone who poses a danger to themselves or others.

I am like the last leaf in autumn
I'm just barely holding on
I can feel the wind blowing past me
It's trying to knock me down
Trying to make me let go
and trying to encourage me

Letting go would mean getting better
Letting go of my past issues, moving on

I am imagining myself being a flower
still in the bud phase
A flower that has dew on it
wanting to open up to the sun

A flower that's just starting

To Love Life

To love life, even when its hardness sits like a broken-
down car in your driveway that no one can afford to fix,
when its hardness sits like a Volkswagen bus,
like the Titanic, like a million-pound cat sitting on you,
on four needle-like legs skewering you to the floor,
like a Boeing 747 has sliced right through you,
when the hardness sits like a waffle iron
on the back of your neck and waits
for the strong-arm seduction of gravity
and plasterboard floors that can't take your weight.
Even when its hardness sits like a titanium wall—
stop shoving. Fly. Go above.

But one day, maybe I will create the map that guides me
through the muck. Maybe I will cut
the invisible, tangled wires that enslave me.
Maybe I will wretch and spit and fall as freely as a bird
shot dead into a screaming plummet to rest.
Or I will live life, not like a shell, but like a success.
Maybe I will scream like a rare, wild bird
and set everything free.
Maybe I'll be there for others. Maybe I'll love someone.
Maybe I will fail, but at least I will have tried.
Maybe I will float into the cold winter sky
carried up by my hopes and desires.

---

6   After "The Thing Is" by Ellen Bass

I Wish I Would Get Old

I wish I would get old
with my hair gray at 20

Will I get a chance to get old?
I want to be the man I want to be
but my anger fills me
They think I'm going to hurt them

The meds they give out
aren't really a part of me
Am I in my own mind
or is it the meds in me?

I want to be my own person
I want to grow old
But will this RAGE let me?

Will these thoughts on paper
show me the way?
I've been struggling since I was 4
Now I'm 17
and 20
seems so far away

Dedicated to my thoughts/the world

Because I Didn't Have that Comfort

HEARTBEAT, NSL
Lily, age 15

Confusion

When I see happy people,
it makes me jealous.
I wish I could be in their shoes,
but I can't.
I'm always confused
because I see people happy
and I don't get why
I can't be.

When I hear stories about people saying
they got abused in whatever way they did,
I don't feel any remorse for them.
I went through it,
so why are you looking for comfort?
I feel like saying, *just get over it
and stop trying to find pity for yourself.*

I know it sounds self-centered
but I've been through hell and back.

I just don't know how to react
when they cry.
I sometimes wish
I could actually feel something for them
and comfort them,
but it seems awkward
and foreign.

So, I just stay and watch
and don't say anything,
and it seems like I'm being rude,
but I'm actually mad that I can't feel anything,
though I try to.
I see it in the community—
why can't I?
Why is it strange to me?

I think it's because
I didn't have that comfort
when I was a child.

Dedicated to anyone

Garbage Can

I feel like a garbage can
People throwing stuff at me
Taking stuff in that might be hard
Not being liked
Being replaced for a better model
Being moved around
Forgotten about

I'd rather be a recycling bin
Finding a better use
Being liked because I'm doing something good
Feeling appreciated
Being something that's cared for
Having stuff that's clean
carefully placed in me

People would know who I am
What I was used for
My purpose in life

The Taste

I have always been   ADDICTED

to something, whether it's   TO

nicotine or coffee, whether
it's   THE

lyrics to a song,
or to the   TASTE

of something new.
I have always been addicted
to the face   OF

my very own   INSANITY.

Addicted

I am addicted to street racing
In my addiction, my life is filled
with loud music, the smell of burning tires
and people who are close enough to be family
but not quite
In my addiction, I am glad to feel like I belong

I am addicted to meth
In my addiction, I hate to think about my mom
because it ruins my high
In my addiction, the real me becomes detached
from reality

I am addicted to my dealers
In my addiction, betrayal comes
in the form of laced drugs
In my addiction, I struggle to stay clean

I am addicted to cutting
In my addiction, I am hiding my arms
In my addiction, I'm in a constant battle
with choosing whether or not to live

I am addicted

How Music Changed My Life

Music has increased my bad habits.
When rap music talks about
drugs, sex, & getting into trouble,
it influences me to lower my guard
& opens me up to risky and dangerous decisions.

Like thinking that
anyone could touch whoever they want.
Like doing street drugs can make you feel better.
Like running away is okay.

What I know to be true is
switching my world around
helps me make better decisions.

Such as walking away from all the drug talk.
Such as not taking certain people's troubling advice.
Such as realizing
I can still love rap & hip hop,
but I know now that I need a change.

Getting Better in the Now

I feel anxious
There are so many people around
all saying that they're here to help us
but it doesn't seem like they help us
It seems like things get worse
whenever they try
Like, if I'm in the QR[7]
they say, *Don't worry, it will get better*
or like if I'm in Juvie
they say, *Don't worry, you'll get out of here soon*
but it never gets better
It seems like it never will

I never want to work on what I need to work on
I need to control my anger
To socialize with people appropriately
I need to learn
to live without using drugs or alcohol
to calm myself or try to make things better
I need to cope
and radically accept the things I cannot change

---

7   Quiet room

I cannot change my ADD and ADHD
I have to learn to cope with my family
even if they are not the family that I wish for
I cannot change the life God gave me
or the past that was given to me

I can only change what's in front of me
Only in this second
I can't go back
and tell my parents not to give me up
Or tell one family to adopt me
and the other, *don't*

My life is screwed up right now
But even in the worst situations
I need to focus
on getting better in the now
without always worrying about what I've done wrong

Dedicated to my life and family

An Explanation

There's just a lot of stuff on my mind
I'm not really sure how to get it all out
I can always try to talk to someone
but people usually seem busy
I feel like they don't have time for me
Everyone seems caught up in their own problems
I try to help other people with their problems
I never really focus on mine

When I look for my problems
they are not that hard to find
They *are* hard to deal with

My problems are a wide range
I deal with stuff like
other kids being dicks
Trying to balance out my schoolwork
Trying not to fall back into drugs
Trying to figure out how to cope
with the grief of losing both my parents

In two days, it will have been a year
since my dad passed away
The hard thing
is that he committed suicide by a drug overdose

I have problems with drugs
and suicidal thoughts
My biggest fear is relapsing
and becoming suicidal again
I don't want to show that as an example for others
I don't want people to think I'm going to die
from a drug overdose like my parents did

It reminds me of how, before rehab
I had people tell me to my face
they don't think I will live past 20
Even random people at school or on the streets
Probably because I was high at the time
Now I'm clean
Now I'm motivated
Now I want to live
Now I have something to live for
That thing is other people
I can care about helping other people
even if I can't help myself

Discharge

When I think of home
I think of the wilderness around me,
friends next to me,
the sensation of my dog's silky fur,
the lathering of shampoo,

scary thoughts of returning to my past
and the dangers it brought me.
There's more to worry about than to look forward to.
The more is not the merrier in this case.

The more that failure brings,
the more I can accomplish
because I'm scared of messing up:

starting drugs and drinking again,
returning to habits I thought I'd forgot.

The worst part
is that I could come close to death again,
as close as I was before.

The best part of discharge
is returning to a place that's simpler than here.
This place is as complex
as a corn maze on Halloween.

Freedom is a complex idea, too.
I know what it feels like to be trapped,
like running a lap that never ends.
Being tired all the time.
I remember what freedom feels like from second grade
when I was unleashed from my father,
able to roam,
and see how life is going to be with my own eyes.

Now I'm being unleashed from CSTC
and going to be free with all of me.
Free to see a new world ahead of me.
A world full of me!

Dedicated to CSTC

I Am Not Afraid to Be Myself

STORY OF MY HEART
Edgar

Far Away

I'm far away from home.
My mom's in crisis, and I can't help her.
She can't find a job because she's illegal.
She's not lazy.

I used to see her when I was a little girl.
She was all burnt and tired and dusty,
sometimes her nose bleeding
from working hours outside in the sun.
I gave her a lot of problems
when I was growing up.
I got raped
and my behavior changed.

She missed a lot of work
because of the appointments I had.
She could have just said
Nah, I'm not gonna take you
but she tried her best.
I started doing drugs
and alcohol,
got involved in a gang
and now all of this affects me
and it affects her.

Now people put her down.
They go against her,
saying she's an irresponsible mom,
but the truth is
she always tried her best,
but I always made her look bad.

She has to go to court today for both of us
where they always mistranslate her words,
where she can't really stand up for herself
because she doesn't know English that good.

I'm worried they'll keep me here longer
and the longer I'm here,
I can't help her.

Trust

Trust is just an illusion
It pokes at you until you bite the bait
Then it strings you along
Just when you think you're in a safe haven
it drops you on your head at the doorstep of hell
Trust is just a waste of time, 'cause no matter what you do
sometimes some wounds
are too deep to bounce back from

Even though they try to trust you, want to trust you
they're still scared
Even though you're trying
Even though you're doing your best
you can't always predict what's going to happen

My parents trusted me to tell them
when it was getting to be too much
but look where I am now
When I go home on pass[8], the doors now all have locks
All the windows are reinforced
because when I get to a certain point
I forget where I am, and I'll do anything to get out
You can't predict what's going to happen
Trust is hard to gain
but easy to lose

––––

8   Youth Residents at CSTC go on "passes" home for periods of time.

Don't Know Why

Shit happens, man
I don't know why, but it just does
One day you're alright
A couple days later
you realize you weren't alright
You get into a cycle
You OD, you go to the hospital
You OD, you go to the hospital
until you don't even know who you are anymore
You're not the kid who loves holidays
and never gets in trouble anymore
Sometimes you don't even care
But sometimes, you wish things had gone differently
It hurts
It hurts a lot
But like I said, shit happens

My "Retard" Button

I knew I was always different
It was hard for me to make friends
and to understand
why people did what they did
Why people felt the way they felt
I didn't like to talk
and I hated looking people in the eyes
I got upset over little things
and people would tell me it was no big deal
but inside, I felt like my world was ending
I've always had these tics
I scratch when I feel nervous
I always play with my hair
and my hands can never stop moving

My doctors say I need to work on it
They say it's not socially appropriate
I didn't understand for the longest time
until they told me I have autism

They explained to me that that was why it was hard
Why I would jump whenever people touched my back
Why kids picked on me
and called me "retard"
Why they would purposely touch my back
and call it my "Retard Button"
because they knew
I would jump

They said that's why it was hard to make friends
and now that I know, I want to fix it
It feels like my brain is broken
I just want to be like everybody else
I asked them if I could have a lobotomy
Maybe that would fix it
But they told me nothing would fix it
because it's just who I am
Just the way I was made
And that's hard for me
because I like to fix things
and this is something I can't fix

So I guess I'll just have to learn to manage it
My brain may be broken
but I'm going to duct tape it back together

Dedicated to my army of minions

The Story of My Heart

It's been working hard all these years.
It's like a door. At first, it was open a lot.
Then someone walked through it
who should have known better.
So my heart decided to stop opening
like a door with attic furniture piled up behind it.

My heart is broken into so many pieces,
nobody will have enough time to heal it.
I've been hurt so much and tried to put back the pieces,
but once I get close, they fall apart
and double.
Sometimes, I feel like my heart
is going to explode
because of how many broken pieces
are inside.

My heart is so big, it needs a five-story mansion.
Sometimes it feels like it's going to burst
out of my chest. My heart is so big,
it needs a SWAT team to protect it.
It could pump the ocean through it.

My heart—
broken, mended, cracked—
spilled into a mud puddle. Muddled,
shredded, grated, waiting for wings,
singing,
but way out of tune.

The story of my heart
is written on invisible pages
soft and fragile as a butterfly sigh.
It speaks between one blink and the next.
The story of my heart is so high and shiny,
only eagles hear it.
Deep and velvety—moles wear it
tunneling home.
The story of my heart
bounces and changes like a Super Ball.
Dreams with me to sleep.
The story of my heart
opens in a place of musical solitude—
angry, buzzing, discordant notes
and soaring rollercoaster scales.
The faces of everyone I know
in a minor key.
My hopes are major,
what happens is accidental.

The Garden of Exquisite Art

Start by looking at a peach blossom.
Imagine yourself as the blossom—
how hard it is to get the sunlight
and how cold it is at night.
Then think of space, uncharted planets
in vibrant colors of blues, greens, yellows...
You can't judge because we're all the same—
exquisite in our own way.
Art is imagination
and imagination is art.

My art is based off my childhood.
I was taken away from my mom
when I was young
and I fought against the police
with a couple of my friends.
Got put in juvenile hall.
Got sentenced to a year there.
I was a very angry kid
with unchartered behavior
and possibilities.

I got put in a mental facility.
The kids drugged me. They beat me.
When I got out, I got into gangs
and drugs,
and I knew that wasn't the thing for me,
but I didn't listen to my heart.

My childhood was excruciatingly painful—
terrorizing.
I got beaten until I was bloody
and then I was put outside to sleep
with nothing but my pajamas
in the snow.

I was put in some bad situations
and with some bad people in foster homes.
And then I turned my life around
by coming to Child Study & Treatment Center.

Art is huge in my life.
It helps me out
by getting my feelings out
into the world.

Dear reader, thank you for reading this.

Words of Wisdom

Eat chicken burgers
because they will improve your immune system
Dance like a pig because it will make you lose weight
Laugh like you have Jell-O below your feet
Talk with passion because you'll gain respect
Be silent so you can clear your mind
and breathe better
First thing when you wake up, eat a banana
because it will keep you young
In the winter of your life, make sure to stay cozy
In the spring of your life, make sure you stretch
and get out
In the summer of your life, make sure you swim
so you can stay healthy
In the autumn of your life, make sure to take walks
When it's raining, make sure you don't forget your humor
When you have a bad day, you can always think
about the times you've helped others

Dedicated to my mom

Euphoria

Surprisingly, scary movies
The adrenaline rush gets me going

Competitive swimming
Water rushing over my face

Running track
All the shiny medals received from wins

Smelling new fragrances of lotions
Like vanilla, like sweet pea and spearmint

Practicing yoga
My back cracking calms my body and mind

Baking delicious desserts
Cupcakes with white and dark chocolate

Relaxing bubble baths
Serenity for my thoughts

Taking time to journal
Feelings can be released onto paper

Dedicated to my brother

How Happy My Life Is

Everything is going well
The world keeps going on for me
I'm living my life to the fullest
I'm happy seeing people I like
I'm not afraid of my treatment anymore
If something tries to ruin my day
I could say that's just the way it is
because when I'm happy, nothing can hurt me
I'm not afraid to be myself
or look out the window to see the sunlight
because I know my future is going to be bright
I'm not afraid to be feminine
knowing that it's just a part of me
and who I am
I'm okay knowing that I can't change
This is how happy my life is

Dedicated to my daddy

Life, Like a Labyrinth

DINOSAURS
Richie

Who am I?

Who am I? I don't know.
People say, *How could you hurt that person so easily?*
How were you so strong that with one hit
you could hurt that person with a bruise?
Every night and day, I think about
who am I really?
I don't remember much of my past life.
People ask me, *Why do your eyes turn jet black at night?*
Why can you see at night?
Why are you more active at night?
When people ask what my favorite food is,
I can't bring myself to say it.
I don't want them to think I'm some sort of freak.
So instead, I lie.
People judge me sometimes for who I am.
Tell me to 'eff off.
I think I'm abnormal.
I think I'm some sort of demon
sent by hell to bring pain to others.
Because the way I act is abnormal
and dangerous for a human.
I'm ashamed of what I've become.

Dedicated to my foster family

Hits

Hit
Take another one
Hit
Another
Hit
Just can't stop taking
Hits
When will I stop taking these
Hits
I guess I'm truly not perfect without my
Hits
Dizzying, spinning like a roller coaster with my
Hits
Calm, organized, and neat without my
Hits
People disapprove when I take
Hits
In my mind, my
Hits

are all I have

Dedicated to my family

Scars

I am the happy one
who likes to draw anime
I am the hyper, crazy one
who plays Black Ops and kills zombies
I am the defiant one
who never follows directions
I am the one with the scars
and their secrets

I am the messed up one
who thinks terrible things when I am angry
I am the helpless one
who can't change my behaviors
I am the hurt one
but much more hurt on the inside
I am the one with the scars
and their angry message
that I've had a terrible life
and want it to be over with

I am the strong one who is determined
to make a book of anime
I am the dreamer who imagines a different life
A time when my life will be perfect
and I am in my happy place

I am the childlike one
who remembers my childhood terrors

I am the one with scars
but they are not me
And one day, their meaning will be
that I am a better person
than I am now

Dedicated to Mom

Tornado of Emotions

I feel scared, alone, mad
anxious, depressed, and confused
I don't understand
what's holding them back
or why I won't express the way I feel

I could probably walk through life
holding a smile for everybody
but on the inside, I'm crashing down
like the towers on 9/11
from the abandonment of my mother
to being trapped in a facility
that tries to get to the core of my problems
but they get stuck at each wall of my heart
like the Great Wall of China

It was so much easier when I was 5 or 6
to explain to my mother that I was sad
Now it seems like a war to get to her
When she finally tries to get me to break
I lock myself in the cold cell of my room

All my emotions are creating a tornado
spinning in circles—juggling one after another
Are my emotions the reason I seclude myself
and feel so alone?
When somebody asks me how I feel
I can't even explain it
It's like you can't explain how birds fly
My emotions are chaining me up
Hiding me from a world of happiness

When I dream of something happy
reality breaks it down
Sometimes I feel scared to be happy
It's like showing the real me that feels weak
People say, *Oh yeah, you can control your emotions anytime*
But my emotions are holding me hostage
like how they keep those animals in cages
How they made innocent people work for them
like the slaves in the South
I don't understand what is holding me back
Is it the emotions
or is it me?

Dedicated to my boyfriend

This Is How to Be Brave

Take off your glasses, let go of being afraid,
run naked in the streets eating cotton candy
while singing your favorite song.
Make a choice to be brave and stick with it.
Face your fears.
Stand up for what you believe in—
with or without support. Don't refuse
to open your eyes. See things for how they really are.
Become the solution to your own fears,
even if it requires all your years.
Try something new. Ask a question. Say nothing.
Love yourself. Love others.
And love society.
I need to be brave to talk to people
about my feelings.
I need to be brave to get my life straightened out
so I can move back home.
Cartwheel. Reel in the wind
of a winter's storm,
eat Theo dark chocolate—
cherries with almonds.
Listen to a quiet cello.

My Deep Sleep Dream

My peaceful place is my dreams—
The moon shines a gloomy shine
on a deep dark forest
where I sit beneath my giant oak tree
and dream of happy moments
like mythical creatures—
Pegasus, dragons, monsters,
cyclops, wizards,
werewolves, and vampires.
I smell the fresh smell of earth
and gloppy smell of the swamp—
a brownish-green.
I smell my dog lying next to me.
I am calm
as a feather flapping in the wind.
I hear deep voices from the forest.
They are talking to me.
They say, *Dream a peaceful dream.*
Sleep a peaceful sleep. Smell a peaceful smell
like earth and flowers and moss.
And dream.
I go to my peaceful place at night.
I sleep.

Family Issues

My mom got kicked out of her house recently
She didn't pay rent for three months
It made me feel sad as pouring down rain
And I was afraid she would get back into drugs
I haven't gotten in touch with her
because she's living in a hotel
I worry a lot because she might get hurt
I remember the time I went to California with my mom
We went on a roller coaster
We were both screaming
but it was awesome

My grandmother's been in and out of the hospital
She's had lots of medical issues, like dementia
The great news is that she might come visit me
on Sunday. It makes me depressed
because she took care of me most of my life.
When I was little, she watched my soccer games
I felt really proud of myself
because she was watching me
and I worked really hard to get to the level I was

I haven't seen my little brother in almost six months
He's in Seattle
I miss him a lot
He lost trust in me
because I got into trouble a lot
and then one day I came home
under the influence
and I hurt him very bad. Then
I went to juvie
and I haven't seen him since
I remember the time we were little
and went to the beach at Ocean Shores
We swam. We talked about our bond
and how we wanted to do this a lot more

Dedicated to my mom, my grandma, and my brother

How I Am

I am the happy girl
who likes to buy perfume
and earrings—hoops as big as peaches.

I am the out-of-control girl
who yells and cries for nothing
and takes things that are not real.
I am the girl who imagines
people are laughing at her,
but they really aren't.

A long time ago,
I wanted to be a different girl.
I wanted to be fat
and I don't know why.

I am the girl who laughs
when my brain reminds me
what I used to do in my room—
scream
while I tried to move the bed.

I am the girl who cried when Immigration
took my dad away to Mexico four years ago.
And when I think about it, I get out of control.
I start to shake and cry.

I am the girl who hopes
that my dad comes back home
because we need him.

Dedicated to Dad

Hey Dad, Listen Up!

Hey Dad, listen up!
Why did you ever go?
You told me when I was 7
that you would come back for me.
You told me that you would never
forget about me.

Hey "Dad," listen up!
Remember how I would always
call people to see where you were?
Remember how I ran away from home
to go find you?
Remember how you were with your other kids
when I did find you, and you told me you were busy?
Well, guess what? I hate you for that!
If you were here right now, I'd probably hit you.
For all the times you cussed me out,
telling me I'm worth nothing
and no one cares.
For treating your girlfriend's kids with more love
even though I was your firstborn!
Maybe you just don't get it though.
I really do love you.
I'm not the one who walked away.

Hey "Dad," listen up!
I'm 14 now. Did you know that?
Do you remember when you asked
my coach when my birthday was?
Do you remember how you would call
Howie on his birthday and
talk to him for hours?
I do, and I hate you for it!
I hope you're doing well now,
sitting in your prison cell.
I hope you're thinking about how to change things.
But maybe you don't even remember me.
But I know you
better than you know yourself.
I hope you're going to try
and see me when you're out. I hope
you'll be doing better.
I want you to know
that I love you,
but hate you also!

Dedicated to my dad

Addicted

I am addicted to knowledge.
In my addiction, my life is filled
with surprises and twists like a labyrinth.
In my addiction, I am glad to feel the essence
of new ideas, better than drugs.
I am addicted to music.
In my addiction, I hate
to think about the dissonance of certain things.
In my addiction, the real me becomes a surfer
riding the sound waves.

I am addicted to my friends.
In my addiction, betrayal comes
in the form of subtle rumors that spread like a plague
and grow in the mind's eye.
In my addiction, I struggle to maintain relationships
like a lone boat in the midst of a tidal wave.

I am addicted to drugs.
In my addiction, I am hiding
my emotional instability & traumas of the past.
In my addiction,
I'm in a constant battle with myself—a catch-22.

To the Labyrinth in My Head

What has caused your intricate paths,
deceptive to those who enter?
Why do you lead me off the path to success?
Where have you led me in the trying times of life?
When will your corrupt amusement end?
Who else have you caused confusion
within their own mind?
How have you not had guilt
in your knowingly mischievous games?

Is it only me you have tortured?
Is it the boredom in this seemingly simple life?
Have you led me to a garden of growth
or a barren wasteland of loss?
Is this never going to end, or is it almost over?
Do you see this as a learning experience
or a way to kill me off?
You must not have guilt, do you?

Honesty

Honesty is the slow flow of an ocean
Sometimes honesty is the hardest thing to say
because you don't know the price you're going to pay
not knowing if it's going to be okay
What does it take for you to be honest?
A million dollars? A new house? For me to be honest
I need the words to come out perfectly. I need my heart
to keep beating *dondondondon*. To be alive
It would be honest to say that my heart
is the thing I don't want to be seen lost in lies
forgotten in the highs
Telling my head and shoulders to rise
but when I look into a mirror
it's not who you think you see
It's everything you wanted me to be
I know honesty is the key
to set me free. Darkness is cavin'
My honest symbol is the raven
It would be a lie for me to tell you
that I love you
but it would be honest for me to say
that I'm scared
Honesty is who I want to be

Just Ordinary, Until...

NIKEPRO
Stephen, age 12

I am

Today, I am a face in the sky
Yesterday, I was a baby
listening to a mother cry
On the street, I am a homeless boy wandering on
In my room, I am a depressed teen
trying to remember I'm a human being
To my mom, I am a dangerous thing
To my dad, I am a punching bag
stuffed with beans
My friends think I am weird
and wrong and can't belong
Really, I am a helpless boy wondering if I belong

An Understanding

To understand me, you would have to go through every step of my despair to feel my pain and suffering. To understand me, you would have to be locked up in a 6x6 cell for six months. You would have to take medications, so you don't kill someone. You would have to be in special facilities for nine years. You would have to be separated from your family for most of your life. You would have to be hardened by seclusion and grown by pain.

Do you understand me?

Dedicated to my sisters

Just Ordinary, Until...

It was just ordinary until
I decided to run away
Found myself hiding
Scared, paranoid
What to do?
Stay here?
Go back?

I don't know what got me to that state
Was it being scared?
Was it something I don't know?
Found myself on a bridge
and plummeted into the highway
straight to hell

I woke up. They were drilling into my leg
My parents next to me crying

That next week and a half? Miserable
Wake up. Shriek in pain
Press a button. Fall asleep laughing

Those next two months in a wheelchair
So many pills. I don't remember
what happened

To this day, I still feel pain
physically
and emotionally
Please, just go away

Dedicated to family and friends

Ode to Jealousy

Oh, jealousy!
I love the way you tangle me up in thoughts,
whether I believe you,
or believe them.

You make me laugh sometimes because you
whisper in my ear,
with the tingling feeling of lies.

You make me want to write a love song to you.
The first line would be,
Oh, jealousy. Oh, jealousy you are super suspicious.

You make me want to dress you up
in rich, vibrant colors—purples
so I can see you lurking near

and whirl you to a faraway land
so I don't have you lurking around anymore.

If I could give you a nickname,
it would be "Treacherous."
You're like a cut in my skin
that sinks like the Titanic—
deeper,
> deeper
>> every second.

If I could wish one thing for you,
it would be
a plane ticket,
so I can get rid of you!

Jealousy, jealousy,
you are gone.

Dedicated to my feelings

Pain

Pain is a word for a person who is afraid
Pain hurts, but you must be better than what pain is

Pain is a monster that brews inside us
Every day, I have Major Pain come to my house
and straighten me up
He is the pain everywhere
like a toothache rotting in my mouth

Pain is in a bullet.
When pain gets to you
you're through

Pain—remember this warning—pain may
hurt but it will make you stronger in everyday life
and if so, the more you get comfortable
the more you see through, the more you fix your issue

The more you look at yourself, the more you feel
The less you feel, the worse it gets

There's a thought in every person's mind before they die
I bet that thought is *I'm a goner*
but we stay strong, we stay brave
We stay holy and never give up
because what's right is what's ours
and honor
and freedom from Major Pain
is all ours

To be continued
                    in the next generation—T, out

Dedicated to everyone

My Way

Why did you go?
Why did you leave me?
Because of you, I grew up without a dad.
I have to wonder why you killed yourself
for the rest of my life.

You taught me one thing
that I will never do.
My mother was left alone
and had to be a father and a mother
to two kids.

My life will never end the way yours did.
I will never leave my family
in that horrible pain.
I refuse to put a hole in my head
like you, Daddy.

Was it what you wanted, Dad?
I will never take my own life like you.
I'm going to live life right—
my way.

Dedicated to my family

The Strength of Changing

I am painting my self-portrait.
For this work, I have chosen
the colors of red, blue, and black.
The blue stands for the times I was bustin'
and protecting my streets.
The red stands for what people call misery and death
but I say it's history.
And the black stands for my stance
of strength in recovery.
The background of my self-portrait
will have God standing right beside me
because my life has been given testimony.
In my self-portrait, I will be holding my life story
because God gave me this story—
the most important thing in my life.
In my self-portrait, my eyes will look like crosses.
When people see my self-portrait,
they will say, *Has she changed!*
I would like to give my self-portrait to anybody
because they will appreciate the way I'm me.
The title of my self-portrait will be
"The Strength of Changing."

Reasons to Love Me

Because I will love you back,
no matter what.
Because I can be sweet and caring
when I work through the bad stuff.
Because I am funny, silly, and cute
to those who care enough to stick with me
until the real me shines through.
My life has fallen apart at the seams,
but I'm better now. I'm happy.
Because I come from a hard life
with a hard family, and I'm strong.

Because I love myself, regardless
of what you think.
I'm good at video games.
I care about my friends and family.
I'm good at cooking bite-sized pizzas.
I whip up the most outrageous
green onion, black olive, and swiss cheese omelet.
I love to listen to rock and roll
really, really loud.
I will accept you for who you are.
My love is unconditional,
and I will love you back.

I love people, especially young ones.
I try to see the bright side of things.
I have a sense of humor that is friendly.
I am a good listener.
I like to try new things
even when they scare me—like bouldering.

I was born!
I may not be perfect,
but I do my best in life.
I appreciate life's complications,
especially complicated feelings.
I help people share their stories.
I laugh. Laughter is a key you can use
to open my heart and find plenty.

I'm kind. Kindness to me brings joy
to people's lives.
I'm confident. I soar with strength
that reaches past each and every tree.
I'm me
and that's really all I want to be.

The Currents of My Emotion

CD OF LIFE
Peter, age 9

You Didn't Believe Me

You didn't believe me
when I said I needed you
I was trying hard not to cry
as you walked away
saying I was a big girl
I shouldn't cry
You didn't believe me
when I said I was in pain
The blood dripping from my open wounds
You screamed, *You a big girl! You shouldn't cry*
You didn't believe me
when I said I wanted to die

The beeping of machines
Me knocked out cold in a hospital bed
You a big girl! You know
what you are doing is stupid
You didn't believe me

The broken mirror
My sad eyes staring back at me
You a big girl! You shouldn't cry
You didn't believe me
when I said I didn't want to cry

I didn't believe myself
when I said
I'm a big girl. I shouldn't cry
If I did, I wouldn't feel my tears
rolling down my cheeks
You didn't believe me
I didn't believe me, either

Starless

                              & quiet

          we tiptoe through the

                             night.

        i crawl in & out

              of my s k i n

becoming & allowing   & creating

                    a new

             life

                    a new

             self

every day & every night

                    you let go

                    and hold on

& I GET LEFT

               naked

               &

               alone

               &

               starless

If You Knew...

You see that I'm fat
That I'm a flirt
But you don't know me

You would know me if
you knew how hard it was to find myself pretty
You knew how I feel sometimes that people don't care
You knew how my dad calls me fat

You see that I swear
That I smoke
But you don't know me

You would know me if
you knew how I truly feel
You knew how I love to cook
You knew how I exercise when I'm upset

My Way

I feel trapped. I can't escape
I want to run away
I take my anger out on walls
It doesn't hurt the wall. It hurts me
My hand's messed up

If the wall could feel
it would feel the same way about me
Mad, furious, enraged
The opposite of happy

If my hand could speak
it would say *It hurts*
and, *Don't punch things*

When I'm mad
I don't feel anything
When I calm down
my hand starts to hurt

Punching is better than cutting
It leaves less scars
If my scars could speak
they'd say, *Don't do it*
Think about what happened last time

They can take my stuff away
but they can't take my fists away

I'll keep fighting
until there's nothing left

I'm fighting to get out of here
For freedom
Not to be locked up

I'm fighting for
things I need
Family
Friends

They need to let me do it on my own
It doesn't feel right

I just want to be left alone
My way

My Life of Colors

My mood stays the same, but the color changes.
I start out white, and then the color changes into black
which usually means I'm starting to get heavy—
heavier than the whole atmosphere.
And then I try to do something to move away from it
because black is not a good sign
because first I start to get stressed
and then tense
and then I tense my muscles
and then I start to get angry
and I start to yell and scream.

After that, the color turns to blue.
Blue means that I'm sad,
as sad as the clouds.
My tears are the color of rain.
The color I turn into next is yellow,
yellow as a sunflower.
Yellow stands for when I'm hungry.
I want to eat food like cheeseburgers and fries
from my favorite place.

These are the colors of my life.

Five Reasons I Want to Be the Son of Poseidon

1. Breathing underwater so I could never drown.

2. Controlling the currents. It would make me feel in control. Instead of hitting people when I don't feel in control, I could soak them with water.

3. Making my own hurricanes. It would make me feel like I could do something big and important. Now, instead of making hurricanes, I throw tantrums when I feel small and unimportant or if somebody pisses me off.

4. Walking on water. If people saw me walking on water, they would think I was a freak. Some people would leave me alone, others would bug me. Those people I would soak with the currents. If people left me alone, I would feel sad, but it would also be a good thing because I need to be alone sometimes.

5. Seeing lots of sights like shipwrecks. I might find some treasure and bring it back up. Then I would be a millionaire. I would save half the money for college and give the other half to the poor.

Things I Would Say to My Mom

If I could go back in time
and meet my 14-year-old mom,
it would be at my grandmother's house.

There's a big TV and brown couches.
The TV would be on, playing MTV.
We both like it.

I would tell her
to leave my dad as soon as possible
and to watch over me, down the road
and to prepare, because there will be bumpy roads.

I wish I could tell her then
to raise me kinda better.
Keep me away from smoking and violence,
so I wouldn't be like I am now.

Keep me away from my dad
because he was abusive.
Stay strong, and don't let him bring you down.

If I told her this,
she would accept it
because she could prepare
for how I am going to be today.

But at first, I don't think she would believe me
about my dad.
But then later on,
she would see how he is toward me.

After I say all this,
she would get up and leave
because she wouldn't listen to a stranger
tell her how her kid is going to be.

Dedicated to my mother

Leaving Ketron Cottage

It's been a long time
I will miss you guys a lot
I will start working on my skills
and I will get better

I am sad that I am leaving
and I will never forget you guys
You have always been the light in my shadow
and lit me up

When I first got here, I was a butthead
I've really changed mentally
I used to hit my mom
and this is the only facility
that I've learned anything at

All the other facilities
just threw me down on a bed
and gave me food
and they forgot I was there
and my mom had to call

But you guys lit up my smile
and you guys changed me
and that helped me a lot

In six months, I will come back
and see how everybody is
and be the best I can be
out in the community

Som times I Fiel Like A Peney

I feel like a penny
Alone
Thrown away
My body ain't worth a penny
I feel like a lost, lonely penny
No one cares about a penny
Pennies are all being thrown away
Pennies are not used very often

I feel like I've just been abandoned by my friend
People are throwing pennies away
saying that they aren't worth much
   That they are garbage

There I lay in the dark
   Waiting to be picked up
   Lying there helpless, motionless
Pennies are being thrown away and not being used

I wait to be used
I wait to be worth something, I wait to be helpful now
   Maybe help kids that have diseases
I could be worth something
Now
I can be helpful

YOUTH ARTIST STATEMENTS[9]

From Ashes *by JANE, age 17*
We can be burned and broken. We can crumble and break. Then, after all the pain, we can grow and bloom out of the dust we were reduced to. I have experienced sexual trafficking, trauma, and abuse, then I grew out of that pain. Yes, it still hurts, but it gets better. Just hold on.

Dedicated to everyone who has been turned to ashes and is learning to grow from them

Heartbeat, NSL *by LILY, age 15*
The remedy of my heart is the healthiness that I am thankful for.

Dedicated to my mother

Story of My Heart *by EDGAR, age 12*
My painting's meaning is to show that love, pride, and feelings do rise, and you can rise and grow with them. So, I'm not about winning the cover art contest. I'm about having fun. All you need to do good art is painting or coloring supplies and most of all— your imagination! As they say, everything you imagine is possible. Thank you!

Dedicated to my moms and brother that always made me laugh

---

9   Listed in order of appearance

Dinosaurs *by RICHIE*
Dedicated to my Dad

NikePro by STEPHEN, *age 12*
Dedicated to my Uncle Patrick. I love him so much!

CD of Life by PETER, *age 9*
When you see the beautiful world around you, take a moment to enjoy it and use it wisely and don't let it go to waste; be happy to see it and you'll have a beautiful life.

Dedicated to my dad, mom, sister, and brother

CPSIA information can be obtained
at www.ICGtesting.com
Printed in the USA
JSHW040833230421
13839JS00003B/12